Riddles Boutique

ISBN: 9781099240447

Table Of Contents

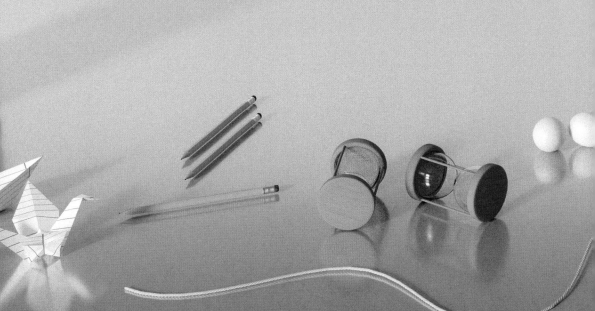

Why Riddles?

First and foremost because riddles are fun.

Riddles are a great way for kids and adults to improve thinking ability and creativity.

Solving problems which may seem un-solvable at a first glance, improves reasoning and problem-solving capacity.

Our minds need to be exercised by something that gives them an opportunity to develop. Activating our brains sharpens our ability to think and improves our learning skills.

The Riddles Boutique is a great way to enjoy some quiet time with family and friends.

How to use this book ?

The Riddles Boutique contains logic designed riddles, one riddle per spread.

As you go through the riddles, take your time, don't rush! Let each riddle gradually sink in, allow it to soak into your brain.

If nothing comes to mind, take a peek at the Tips section to get a hint.

Eventually read the detailed answer, understand it, learn from it....

Test yourself again after a few weeks and find that "What we learn stays forever".

Good luck and have fun

Tip: page 74, Answer: page 86

8

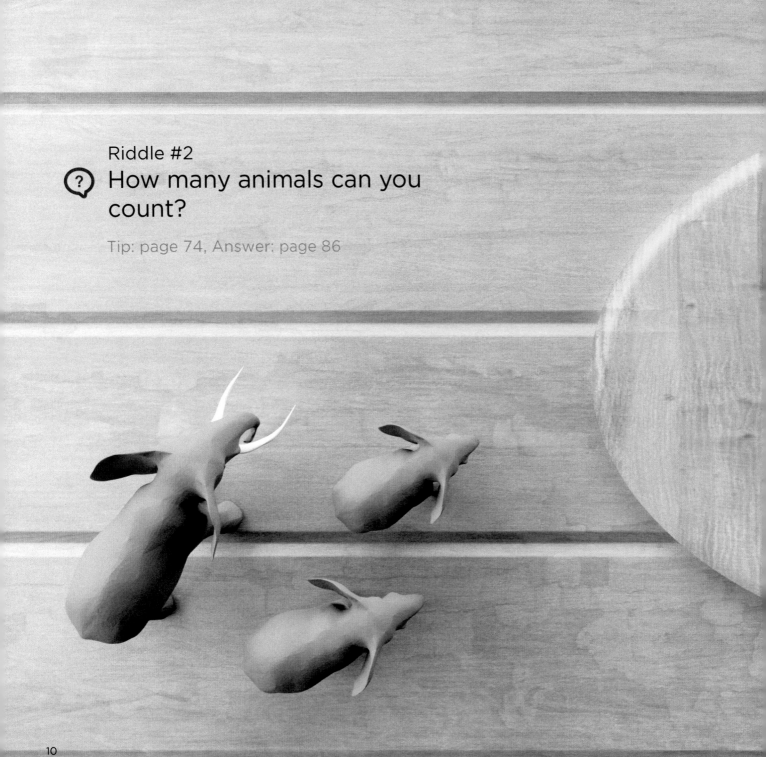

Riddle #2

How many animals can you count?

Tip: page 74, Answer: page 86

Riddle #3

 A microbe duplicates itself
every second.
In one minute it fills a glass.
How long would it take to fill
half a glass ?

Tip: page 74, Answer: page 87

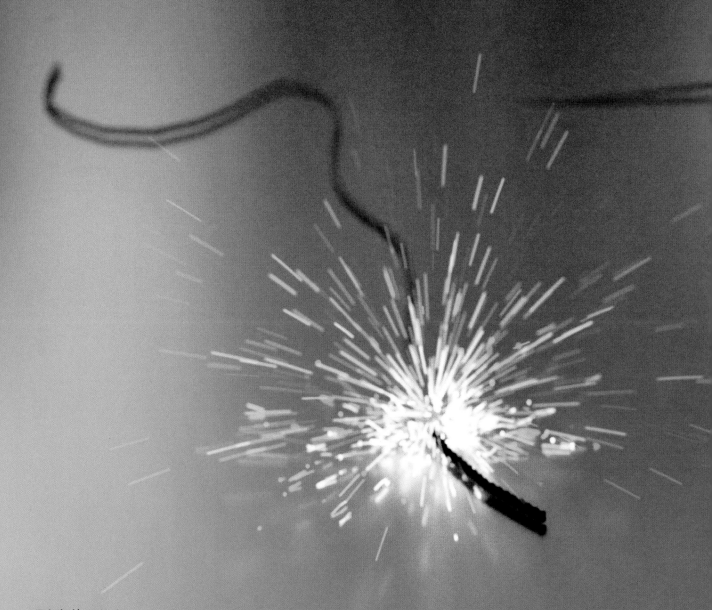

Riddle #4

You have 2 pieces of rope, each burns unevenly from one end to the other in exactly 30 minutes. Can you find a way to time 45 minutes?

Tip: page 74, Answer: page 87

Riddle #5

How many watermellons
are in the pile ?

Tip: page 75, Answer: page 88

Riddle #6

Can you cut the cake
into 4 equal pieces?

Tip: page 75, Answer: page 88

Riddle #7

 How many pencils hold the pencil statue ?

Tip: page 75, Answer: page 89

Riddle #8

Given 9 identical sacks, 8 contain silver coins and one contains heavier gold coins. Can you find the gold sack with only two measuring scales?

Tip: page 75, Answer: page 89

Riddle #9

 How many cubes are on the table ?

Tip: page 76, Answer: page 90

? Can you arrange six popsicle sticks to
form 4 equilateral triangles ?

Tip: page 76, Answer: page 90

Riddle #11

Can you find a path for each ant to get to it's flag, without crossing each others' trails ?

Tip: page 76, Answer: page 91

Riddle #12

 You have 5 gallon and 3 gallon water jars, but need exactly 4 gallons of water. Can you fill the jar with exactly 4 gallons of water ?

Tip: page 77, Answer: page 91

3 GALLON

Pure Water

With a heritage that dates back to 1894, it derives its name from the
natural arrowhead formation that points to the water.

5 GALLON

Pure Water

With a heritage that dates back to 1894, it derives its name from the
natural arrowhead formation that points to the water.

Riddle #13

? How many triangles can
you count ?

Tip: page 77, Answer: page 92

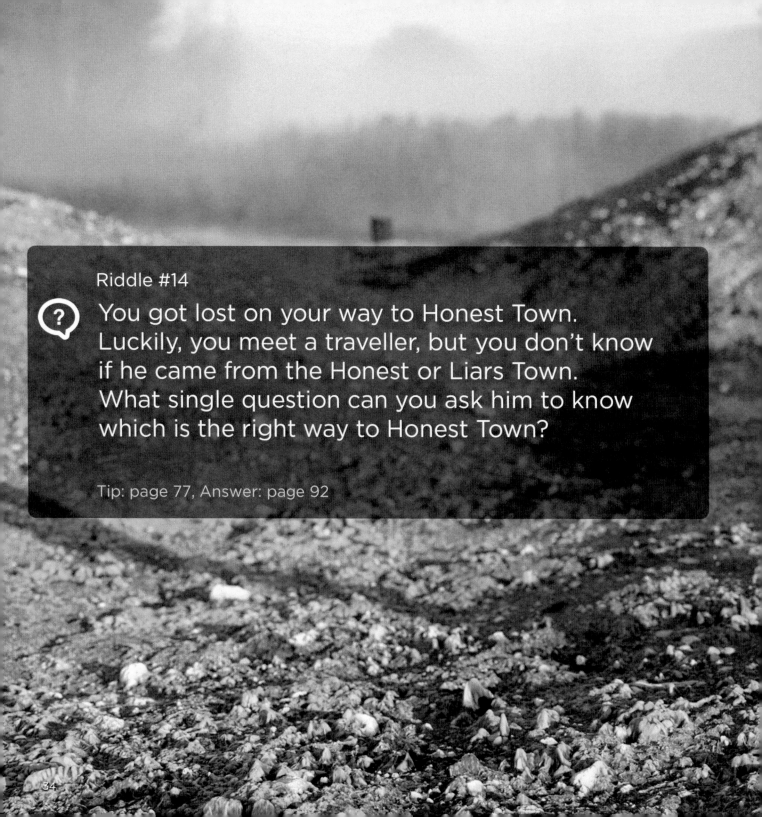

Riddle #14

You got lost on your way to Honest Town. Luckily, you meet a traveller, but you don't know if he came from the Honest or Liars Town. What single question can you ask him to know which is the right way to Honest Town?

Tip: page 77, Answer: page 92

? Can you connect these 9 dots with four straight lines, and <u>without</u> lifting the pencil off the paper?

Tip: page 78, Answer: page 93

Riddle #16

Knights of the round table had a game: two players, each would place a coin on the round table, in a way that doesn't collide with any other coin.

The knight that has no place to position the next coin - loses.

Asuminging you're a knight, and have the first move - can you think of a way by which you'll always win?

Tip: page 78, Answer: page 93

Riddle #17

? Perfectly cooked eggs are boiled for exactly 3 minutes. You have a 5 minute and a 2 minute timer, can you find a way to perfectly boil the eggs?

Tip: page 78, Answer: page 94

Riddle #18

? Climbing this sharp 500 feet cliff is tough. You climb 100 feet but drop 50 on each day. How many days would it take you to reach the top ?

Tip: page 78, Answer: page 94

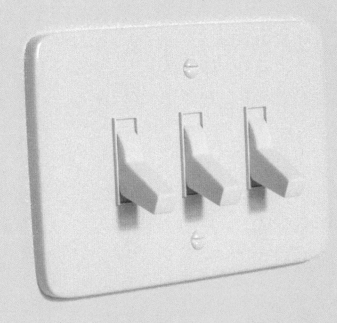

Riddle #19

There is one lightbulb inside the closet, controlled by one of those switches. Can you figure out which one is it, by opening the closet doors only once ?

You can play with the switches as much as you like, before opening the door.

Tip: page 79, Answer: page 95

Riddle #20

? What's the largest amount of money you can have in change and still not have change for a dollar?
(Penny, Nickel, Dime, Quarter)

Tip: page 79, Answer: page 95

Riddle #21

? You have a dime and a dollar, you buy a bat and a ball, the bat costs a dollar more than the ball, how much is the ball?

Tip: page 79, Answer: page 96

The Riddle Boutique

Growing Knowledge

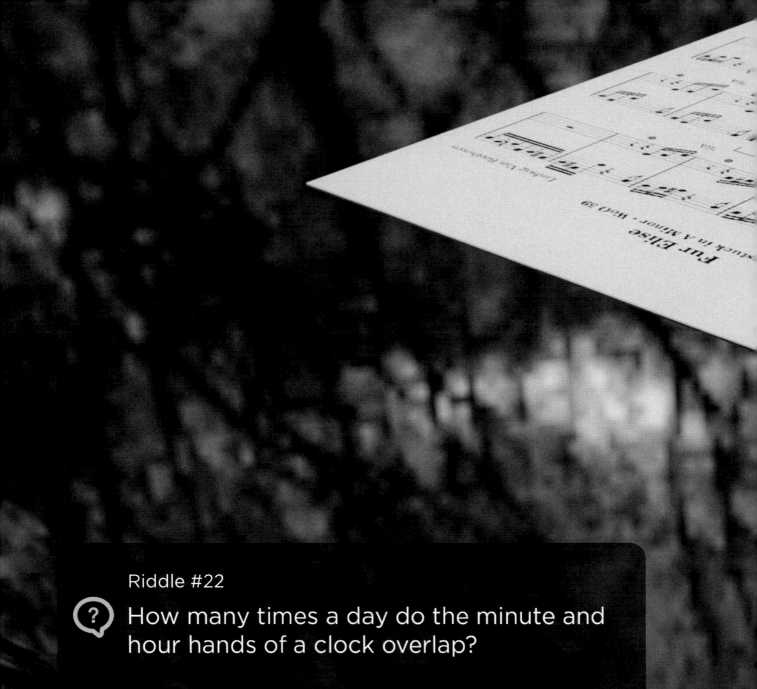

Riddle #22

How many times a day do the minute and hour hands of a clock overlap?

Tip: page 79, Answer: page 96

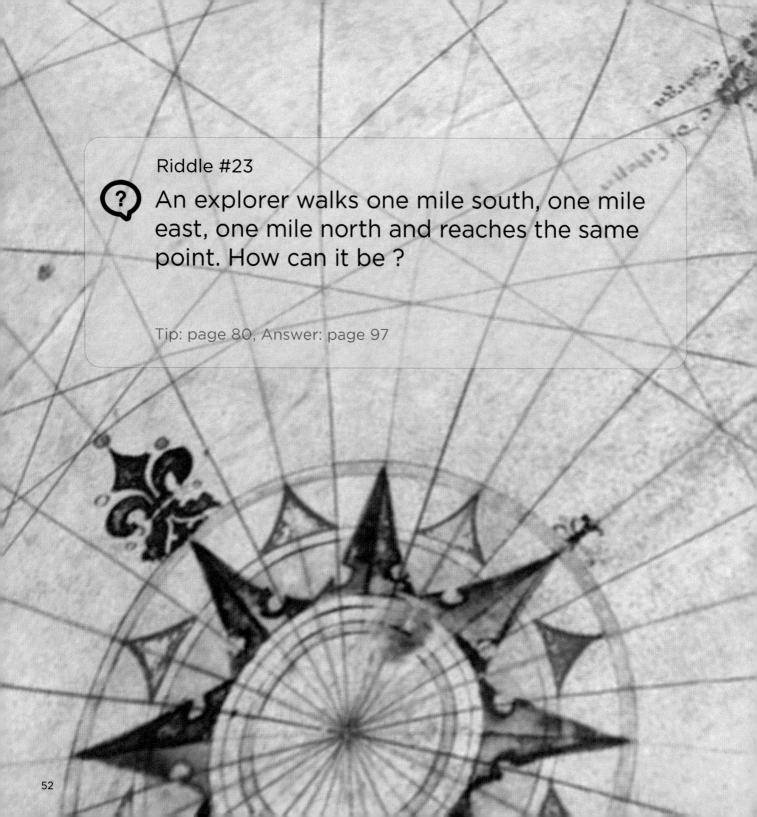

Riddle #23

An explorer walks one mile south, one mile east, one mile north and reaches the same point. How can it be ?

Tip: page 80, Answer: page 97

52

Riddle #24

? Can you place 31 dominoes of size 2×1 blocks on a standard 8×8 chessboard without using the two diagonally opposite black corners ?

Tip: page 80, Answer: page 97

 You need to pour exactly half of the magic red potion into the bowl.
The bottle has a funky shape, it's not symmetrical.
Luckily, you also have a simple marker.
How can you pour exactly half of the potion?

Tip: page 80, Answer: page 98

Riddle #26

Can you get the ball without getting wet ?

The distance between the Island to the edges is 10 foot, you have two wooden blocks which are 9.8 foot each.

Tip: page 80, Answer: page 98

10 foot

9.8 foot

10 foot

Riddle #27

How can you cut a round gouda cheese to eight equal slices? When all you have is three straight cuts to make.

Tip: page 81, Answer: page 99

Riddle #28

? The candy jar contains 30 orange candies, 20 red candies, and 10 blue candies.
When blindfolded, how many candies do you need to take out, to make sure you'll get at least one **blue** candy ?

Tip: page 81, Answer: page 99

Riddle #29

As the turtle walks and turns the wheels, will the bucket on the right move up or down ?

Tip: page 81, Answer: page 100

Riddle #30

A man has to take a wolf, a sheep, and some cabbage across a river.
The boat is tiny and can only carry one passenger at a time. If he leaves the wolf and the sheep alone together, the wolf will eat the sheep. If he leaves the sheep and the cabbage alone together, the sheep will eat the cabbage.
How can he bring all three safely across the river?

Tip: page 81, Answer: page 100

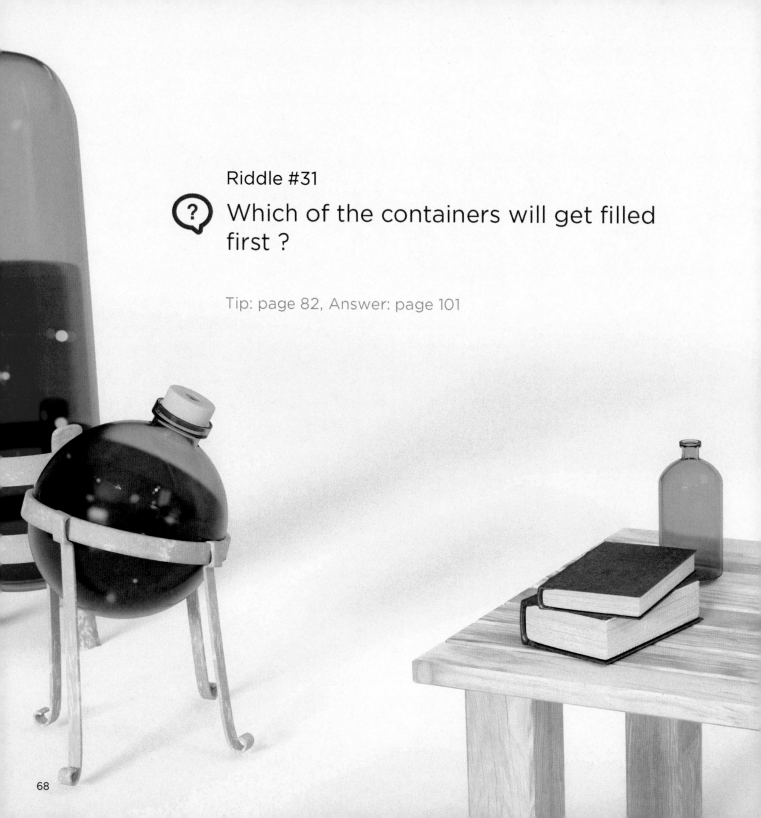

Riddle #31

? **Which of the containers will get filled first ?**

Tip: page 82, Answer: page 101

Riddle #32

? The Romans had a secret Numbers Maze.
You start from the green square, on each step you must move horizontally or vertically exactly the number of squares the block you are currently on, indicates.
For example - from the green block, you can move one block right or up.
What steps do you need to take to get to the red X, on the top right corner?

Tip: page 82, Answer: page 101

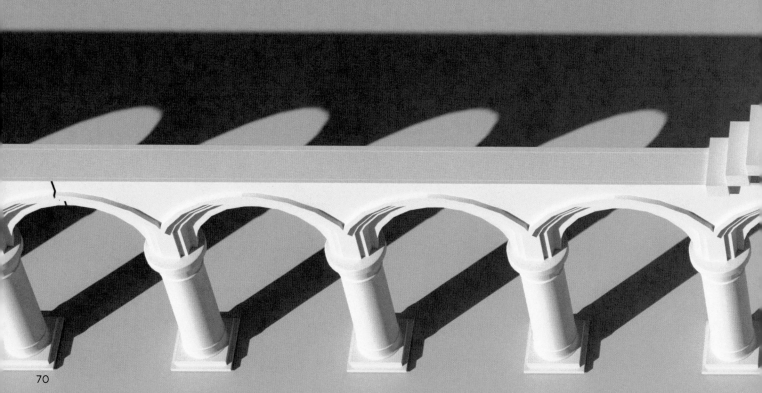

Keep Thinking
You can do
it!

Take Your
Time

Don't
Rush

- Tips -

Riddle #1
Notice the mirror reflects some of the marbles on the table!

page 10

Riddle #2
If you'll look closely, you'll notice animals crafted within each other, search carefully for animals within other animals!

page 12

Riddle #3
The answer is not 30 seconds!
The microbe DOUBLES ITSELF EVERY SECOND.
Think how the glass would change every second, and specifically think about the last few seconds.

page 14

Riddle #4
Since the ropes do not burn evenly, you can't simply wait for half a rope to burn and measure when 15 minutes have passed! What will happen if you light both ends of one of the ropes?

- Tips -

page 16

Riddle #5
If you'll look closely, you'll see the watermelon pile has the shape of a square pyramid. Try to count how many watermelons are in each of the layers.

page 18

Riddle #6
As a helper, draw a grid of 12 equal squares on the shape.

Since you're looking for 4 equal shapes, 12 divided by 4 is 3. can Do you come up with a shape built from 3 squares that repeats itself?

page 20

Riddle #7
Counting all the pencils is very confusing, look for some pattern, you'll notice the pencils are organized in a few hexagons, start by counting the number of pencils in one of the hexagons.

page 22

Riddle #8
As a first step, weigh two groups of three sacks.

- Tips -

Riddle #9
Not a hard one, simply count the blocks

Riddle #10
Think in a three-dimensional space:

Riddle #11
For simplicity, re-draw the riddle on paper, and start by connecting the red ant to its flag

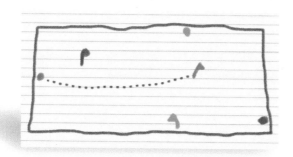

- Tips -

page 30

Riddle #12
Since you can pour water from one Jar to the other, the solution is similar to doing basic math calculations:

5 – 3 = 2
3 – 2 = 1
5 – 1 = 4

page 32

Riddle #13
Notice you can count combinations of triangles that forms triangles as well!

page 34

Riddle #14.
Think of a question you can ask the traveller, whether he's an honest person or a liar, but in any case would give the same answer.

- Tips -

Riddle #15
There's no restriction in continuing a straight line outside the dots, as a hint, start with the following line:

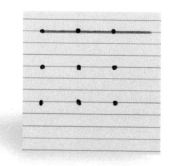

Riddle #16
Notice that you're first, as a hint, place the first coin in the middle, from this point, think symmetry.

Riddle #17
You have a 5 minute and a 2 minute timer – notice the simple math: five minus two equals three.

Riddle #18
The answer is not 10 days, but close ...

- Tips -

page 44

Riddle #19
As a direction ask yourself what does a lightbulb emits other than light ?

page 46

Riddle #20
The answer is an amount that is higher than a dollar!
Start with Quarters, and ask how many you can have, without having change for a dollar, then add dimes, nickels and pennies?

page 48

Riddle #21
The answer is not a dime! If a ball would have cost a dime, the bat would have cost a dime and a dollar, therefore both would have cost a dollar and 20 cents.

page 50

Riddle #22
Imagine the big hand and the minute hand rotating. Find when they are intersecting one another.

- Tips -

Riddle #23
There's only one starting location on earth where this can be true...

Riddle #24
The answer for this one is no, you cannot! The real question here is why? How can you prove it can't be done.
Notice each domino block will always cover one black and one white areas.

Riddle #25
The shape of the bottle is asymmetrical, meaning you can't know where the middle is. But, you can hold the bottle and flip it around, draw lines on it...

Riddle #26
The distance between the island and the edge is larger than the length of the wooden block, when trying to place the wooden block in a straight line it will fall into the pool.
Try to position one of the wooden blocks in a diagonal position.

- Tips -

Riddle #27
Making three straight cuts in a pizza way, will result in six slices only. Can you find a way to make two cuts, get four slices but then cut each into half within a single slice ?

Riddle #28
To provide the right answer, think of the worst case, where as long as there are non-blue candies in the jar, those are the ones you'll take out.

Riddle #29
Follow the direction that the wheels will spin. Start from the left most wheel, gradually advance to the wheel that controls the rope of the bucket.

Riddle #30
As a hint, know you can take a passenger to the other side of the lake, but you can also take him back!

- Tips -

page 68

Riddle #31
Imagine the liquid filling the jars, flowing from one jar to the next. With that in mind, find out which jar will fill first.

page 70

Riddle #32
Try to remember where you've already visited and got stuck. For more help, try to solve it backwards: start from the red square and ask from where it can be reached, do the same from the square you've found, ask from where it can be reached, and so on.

- Answers -

page 8

Riddle #1 - There are 6 marbles on the table

page 10

Riddle #2 - Elephant, Gorilla, Horse, Dog, Cat, Mouse

- Answers -

page 12

Riddle #3 – 59 seconds
Since it takes 60 seconds to fill the glass, and the microbe duplicates itself every second, one second before the glass is full the microbe would fill half a glass, therefore 59 seconds.

57 Seconds   58 Seconds   59 Seconds   60 Seconds

Half glass filled

page 14

Riddle #4
Shape one of the ropes as a circle, connect it's edges to the second rope. Light the other edge of the second rope – it will take it 30 minutes to burn, and then it will light the circle shaped rope – as the rope fully burns – 45 minutes passed.

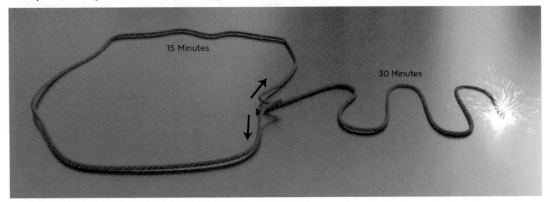

15 Minutes

30 Minutes

- Answers -

page 16

Riddle #5 - There are 30 watermelons in the pile

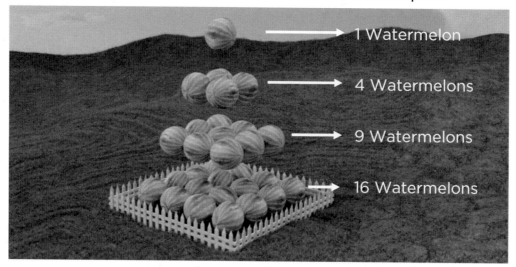

1 Watermelon

4 Watermelons

9 Watermelons

16 Watermelons

page 18

Riddle #6 – Cut the shape as shown below:

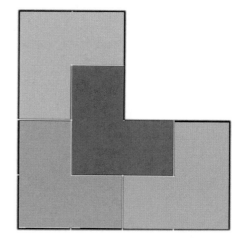

- Answers -

page 20

Riddle #7 - There are 72 pencils in the pencils statue
4 hexagons of pencils, with 18 pencils each:

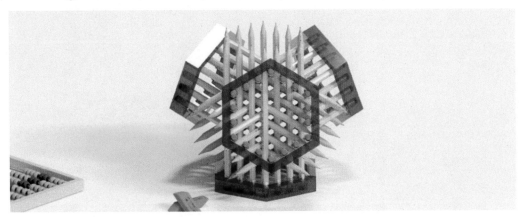

page 22

Riddle #8
Yes, with two scales you can find the golden sack:

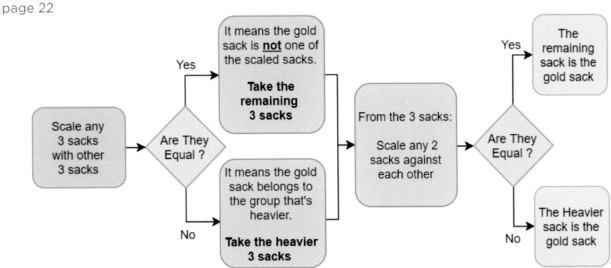

Scale any 3 sacks with other 3 sacks

Are They Equal ?

Yes → It means the gold sack is **not** one of the scaled sacks. **Take the remaining 3 sacks**

No → It means the gold sack belongs to the group that's heavier. **Take the heavier 3 sacks**

From the 3 sacks: Scale any 2 sacks against each other

Are They Equal ?

Yes → The remaining sack is the gold sack

No → The Heavier sack is the gold sack

- Answers -

page 24

Riddle #9 – There are 11 cubes on the table:

page 26

Riddle #10
Build a pyramid from the six popsicle sticks to form 4 equilateral triangles:

- Answers -

page 28

Riddle #11
The dotted lines shows the path of each of the ants.

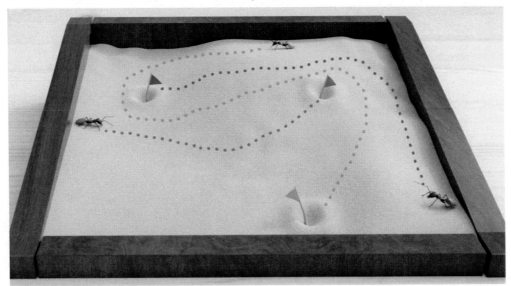

page 30

Riddle #12

Step I	-	Fill the *5-gallon* jar with water
Step II	-	Pour water from the *5-gallon* to the *3-gallon* jar. The *5-gallon* jar will be left with 2 gallons of water.
Step III	-	Empty the *3-gallon* jar, pour the 2 gallons to it.
Step IV	-	Fill the *5-gallon* jar with water
Step V	-	Pour water from the *5-gallon* jar (which is full) to the *3-gallon* jar (which has 2 gallons of water) When the *3-gallon* jar is full, 1 gallon of water was poured to it, leaving the *5-gallon* jar with exactly **4 gallons** of water.

- Answers -

page 32

Riddle #13 – Total 27 Triangles

The diagram bellow marks each of the triangles:

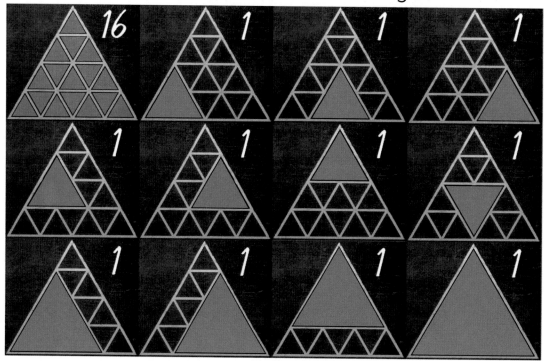

page 34

Riddle #14

Simply ask the person: **"Which town did you come from"**.
If that person is honest – he'll point to the honest town.
If that person is a liar - he'll point to the honest town as well!

- Answers -

page 36

Riddle #15

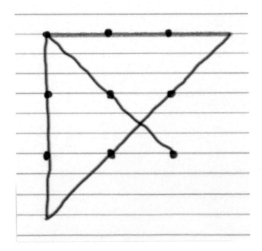

page 38

Riddle #16
Place your first coin in the middle of the table!
From that point, wherever your opponent places the coin, place your coin in the exact opposite symmetrical location. Since the table is symmetrical, it guarantees as long your opponent has a place for his coin, so will you, and therefore you will win.

- Answers -

page 40

Riddle #17
In order to cook the eggs for exactly 3 minutes, **start both timers together.** When the 2-minute-timer is done, place the eggs in the boiling water. The other 5-minute-timer will have exactly 3 minutes left, since 5-2=3. Take the eggs out exactly when the 5-minute-timer is done.

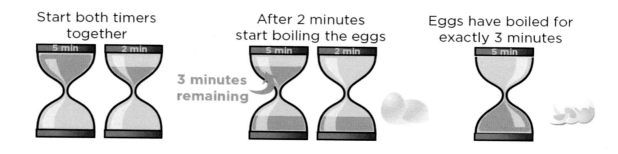

page 42

Riddle #18 - You will reach the top after 9 days
Since in the last climbing day you don't drop!

Day 1 – Reach 100 feet, drop 50 – end at 50 feet
Day 2 – Reach 150 feet, drop 50 – end at 100 feet
Day 3 – Reach 200 feet, drop 50 – end at 150 feet
Day 4 – Reach 250 feet, drop 50 – end at 200 feet
Day 5 – Reach 300 feet, drop 50 – end at 250 feet
Day 6 – Reach 350 feet, drop 50 – end at 300 feet
Day 7 – Reach 400 feet, drop 50 – end at 350 feet
Day 8 – Reach 450 feet, drop 50 – end at 400 feet
Day 9 – Reach 500 feet

- Answers -

page 44

Riddle #19
The physical principle which is used to solve the problem is the fact that a light bulb emits light and also creates heat!

Do the following:
Turn on the first switch and wait for a few minutes, turn it back off. Then turn on the second switch and immediately open the closet door.
If the light is on, the second switch controls the light, if the light is off, touch the lamp, if it's warm, the first switch controls the light and if it's cold the last switch controls the light.

page 46

Riddle #20
You can have $1.19, but still have no change for a dollar

3 Quarters – equals $0.75
4 Dimes – together equals $1.15
4 Pennies - together equals $1.19

Riddle #21

page 48

The bat costs $1.05 (a dollar and a nickel) and the ball costs $0.05 (a nickel)

Bat + Ball = $1.1
Bat – Ball = $1

Bat = $1.05
Ball = $0.05

Riddle #22 - The hands overlap 22 times in a day.

page 50

The hands of a clock overlap 11 times in every 12 hours (Since between 11 and 1, they overlap only once, i.e. at 12 o'clock). The hands overlap about every 65 minutes, not every 60 minutes.

All overlaps within 12 hours

- Answers -

page 52

Riddle #23
The only place on earth were this would be possible is the North Pole.

page 54

Riddle #24
The puzzle is impossible to complete. A domino placed on the chessboard will always cover one white square and one black square. Therefore, a collection of dominoes placed on the board will cover an equal numbers of squares of each color. If the two black corners are removed from the board, then 30 black squares and 32 white squares remain to be covered by dominoes, therefore impossible.

- Answers -

page 56

Riddle #25

Pour some of the lotion into the bowl, using the marker, draw a line on the bottle at the lotion height. Now turn the bottle upside down and once again draw a line on the bottle at the lotion height.

Repeat this process, when the two lines meet, you have poured exactly half of the lotion into the bowl.

page 58

Riddle #26

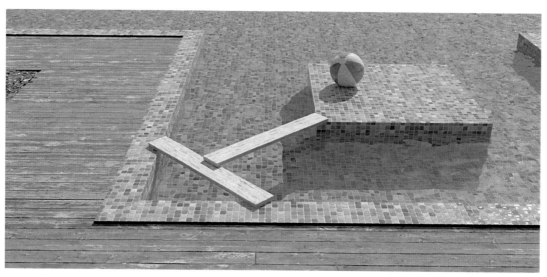

- Answers -

page 60

Riddle #27
Cut the cheese to four slices with two straight cuts, and then cut the cheese horizontally from the side all the way across – to cut each quarter into two, resulting in eight slices with only three cuts.

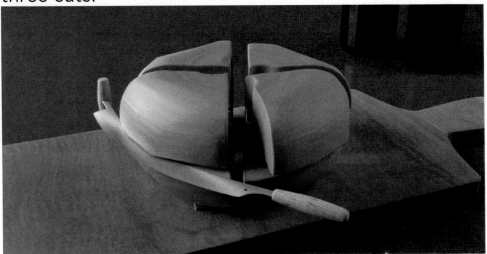

page 62

Riddle #28 – You'll have to take out 51 candies
Since you can't see, you can't tell what color of candy you're fetching each time. The worst case would be, if every fetch you'll take a candy which won't be a blue one. You'll get all the orange and red candies and only then a blue candy. Since there are 30 orange candies and 20 red candies – it would take 51 candies to take out to be sure you finally have a blue candy.

- Answers -

page 64

Riddle #29 - The bucket will move up

page 66

Riddle #30

Step I - Take the sheep to the other side and return.

Step II - Take the cabbage to the other side, but don't leave them both there, **take the sheep back with you**.

Step III - Leave the sheep, and take the wolf to the other side and return.

Step IV - Take the sheep to the other side.

- Answers -

page 68

Riddle #31 – The middle jar would fill up first

Riddle #32

page 70

Thanks to my family and beloved grandfather
who always puzzled us with riddles

ABOUT

The Riddles Boutique came to life through two passions I have in life:
Riddles and 3D modeling

All images in the book were generated with Blender ,a professional, free and open-source 3D computer graphics software toolset used for creating animated films, visual effects, art, 3D printed models, interactive 3D applications and video games.

Thank you for an amazing 3D community and support.

A few models and design credits:
Baseball: UP3D https://up3d.de/
Watch: CVETKO https://www.blendswap.com/blends/view/85648
Compass: HERBERT123 https://www.blendswap.com/blends/view/75033
Knights: mishanay_cool https://free3d.com/3d-model/knight-84265.html

Have comments or suggestions?
Please don't hesitate to contact me at:
riddles-boutique@gmail.com

Hope You Enjoyed

The best way to thank an author is to write a review, Please open Riddles Boutique Amazon page to add your review.

Sincerely *Eran Cohen*

Remember

"*What we learn stays with us forever*"

Made in the USA
Middletown, DE
11 December 2019